My First Bilingual Book · Mon pre... ...ngue

Family

La famille

English-French · Français-anglais

A child's first book of words and fun – in two languages!
Un livre bilingue, rempli de mots et de plaisir pour les tout-petits!

mother

la mère

father

le père

parents

les parents

sister

la sœur

brother

le frère

grandmother

la grand-mère

grandfather

le grand-père

grandparents

les grands-parents

aunt

la tante

uncle

l'oncle

cousins

les cousins et cousines

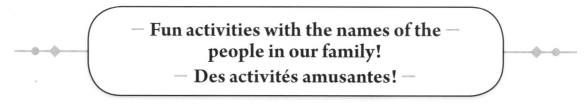

Fun activities with the names of the people in our family!
— Des activités amusantes! —

Can you say the names for these people in your family, in both French and English?
Nomme en français et en anglais tous les membres de la famille qui sont présentés ici.

Say the name of these family members and find their picture in the book.

Prononce les mots que tu vois ici
et retrouve les personnes correspondantes dans le livre.

parents	**cousins**	**aunt**	**grandparents**
les parents	**les cousins et cousines**	**la tante**	**les grands-parents**